One Life to Lose for My Country"

he Arrest and Execution of Nathan Hale

Holly Cefrey

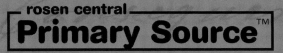

rosen central
Primary Source™

The Rosen Publishing Group, Inc., New York

Published in 2004 by The Rosen Publishing Group, Inc.
29 East 21st Street, New York, NY 10010

Editor: Shira Laskin
Book Design: Erica Clendening
Photo Researcher: Rebecca Anguin-Cohen
Series Photo Researcher: Jeff Wendt

Photo Credits: Cover (left), title page, p. 29 Nathan Hale to Enoch Hale: Autographed Letter, signed
3 June 1776, Yale University Library, May 1954; cover (right) illustration © Debra Wainwright/The
Rosen Publishing Group; pp. 6, 10 from *Nathan Hale: The Ideal Patriot*, Funk and Wagnalls Company, 1902;
p. 14 © Bettmann/Corbis; p. 18 The Granger Collection, NY; p. 22 © North Wind Picture Archives;
p. 30 National Archives and Records Administration; p. 31 © Profiles in History/Corbis;
p. 32 courtesy of the Antiquarian and Landmarks Society, Hartford, CT

First Edition

Library of Congress Cataloging-in-Publication Data

Cefrey, Holly.
   One life to lose for my country : the arrest and execution of Nathan
   Hale / Holly Cefrey.— 1st ed.
      p. cm. — (Great moments in American history)
   Summary: As he awaits execution, American patriot and Revolutionary War
   army captain Nathan Hale recounts his spy mission, arrest by the British
   army, and trial and sentence.
   ISBN 0-8239-4371-2 (lib. bdg.)
   1. Hale, Nathan, 1755-1776—Juvenile literature. 2. United
   States—History—Revolution, 1775-1783—Secret service—Juvenile
   literature. 3. Spies—United States—Biography—Juvenile literature.
   4. Soldiers—United States—Biography—Juvenile literature. [1. Hale,
   Nathan, 1755-1776. 2. Spies. 3. United States—History—Revolution,
   1775-1783—Secret service.] I. Title. II. Series.

E280.H2C44 2003
973.3'85'092—dc21
                                                      2003002689

Contents

Preface

The American Revolutionary War was the fight between American colonists and England. The colonists believed that America should not be controlled by England. They decided to fight for their freedom. There were many more British soldiers than there were American soldiers. The British army, led by General William Howe, was very strong. The British thought they would easily beat the colonists.

The Americans who wanted to be free from England were called patriots. Patriots fought hard to help America win the Revolutionary War. The war lasted from 1775 to 1783.

Controlling the area of New York was important for the British. In July 1776, the British army took over Staten Island. Then, on August 27, General Howe and his troops attacked

American soldiers in the Battle of Long Island. The British won the fight and the Americans were forced back to New York City. The patriots needed to find out what the British army was planning to do next.

Nathan Hale was a patriot and a captain in the American army. Hale was sent on a secret mission to find out what the British were planning. He left New York City in early September to spy on the British troops. However, on September 21, 1776, the British captured Hale. The next day, he was hanged.

Nathan Hale gave his life in the American fight for independence. Imagine his final days as a colonist soldier. What were the thoughts that ran through his mind while he was on his mission—or in the moments just before he was hanged?

Only Captain Hale could tell us his story....

On September 21, 1776, Nathan Hale was captured by British soldiers. This drawing by William Robinson Leigh was originally in black and white and appeared in *Nathan Hale: The Ideal Patriot* in 1902.

Chapter One

LETTERS OF GOODBYE

The sun has come up and the morning light shines on the wall. I have spent a sleepless night in this British jail in New York City. I walked back and forth most of the night, for I knew it would be my very last. I will be put to my death before this new day is finished.

As I sit in this jail, I feel some peace knowing that I will die serving my country. I may have lived only twenty-one years, but I have helped my fellow patriots. I have played my part in our fight for independence. How I hope for a free America!

I have been treated poorly by the British since I was captured. I am under the watch of a very cruel man, William Cunningham. Cunningham is in charge of the jail and is well known for his hatred

of patriots. He yells at me, saying that the British troops will win the war.

The officer watching my jail cell is Captain John Montresor. He is not cruel like Cunningham. Montresor gave me a pen and ink to write my last letters. As I now write to my family and my fellow soldiers, I say goodbye for the last time. I tell them that I know my life is not a wasted thing. I write about how much I believe in our few, proud soldiers. They will not give up until America is free from England's rule. I will die today knowing that another patriot will take my place and carry on our important fight.

After I finish my letters, I hand them to Captain Montresor. "Thank you for your kind-ness, Captain," I say. As I speak to him, I hear soldiers outside, talking as they prepare the rope from which I will be hanged. I will not let myself feel sad.

Montresor turns to leave and promises, "I will pass these on to William Cunningham."

I am happy my words will reach the people I cannot say goodbye to.

Out in the field, I hear Cunningham's unkind voice. Captain Montresor tells him that my last wish is to have my letters sent to my family and freinds. Then it is quiet. I begin to worry. I try to hear what's happening. Suddenly, I hear paper being ripped. The sound is like a knife through my heart. Cunningham has destroyed my letters!

Cunningham shouts, "Must we show how proud this man is to die for his country? Our men must never know the courage of this patriot!" My heart sinks to my stomach. Now my fellow soldiers will never know how my life ended behind enemy lines. My family will not know how proud I am to be a Hale. Cunningham has taken my words, but I will not let him take my pride. I promise myself that I will die with my head held high!

In early September 1776, Commander Washington and Hale discussed Hale's mission to spy on British troops on Long Island. Artist William Robinson Leigh also did this drawing in black and white for *Nathan Hale: The Ideal Patriot*.

MEETING COMMANDER WASHINGTON

I am a prisoner in my own land, I think as I sit in my cell. It is hard to believe. Not long ago, the American army controlled this whole area. We were preparing against a British attack on New York City. The British were stationed on Staten Island and Long Island. British General Howe wanted his men to take control of New York City. He was planning to attack harbor cities to bring them under British control. My commander, George Washington, did not know when or how the British would attack. What he *did* know was that it was only a matter of time before Howe struck.

My mission was to find out as much as I could about the British attack. With this knowledge, we

could win the next battle. We could make sure we were ready to fight and save New York City. We could even catch General Howe and his troops and win the war. I was greatly honored to serve my country in this way.

I remember the day I met with Commander George Washington to discuss my mission. He called for me to come to his headquarters. He told me what I was to do.

Washington smiled and said to me, "Captain Hale, we are pleased that you have offered yourself for this most important position. It is a great favor that you do for our cause."

It was hard to believe that I was speaking with the great Commander Washington. As he spoke, I understood why so many people believed he was the father of the American spirit. I understood why he was chosen to lead our fight against the British. I looked into his eyes that day and saw great courage. I wanted to help this great man protect America.

Commander Washington wanted to know about me. He asked me about my past. I told the commander that I had learned about the British in college. I learned that the British did not treat colonists fairly. Washington also wanted to find out about my work before I was an officer in the American army. I told him that when the fighting began in 1775, I was working as a teacher in Connecticut. But the call for freedom was strong. I stopped teaching and joined the patriot army. I asked my friends to do so as well, and many did. I told Washington I believed that every man was an important part of our fight to be free.

As I left the commander, he firmly shook my hand. "Good luck to you, Captain Hale. The patriots are proud to have you take this mission," he said. I quietly left him, hoping that one day I would again meet this great man.

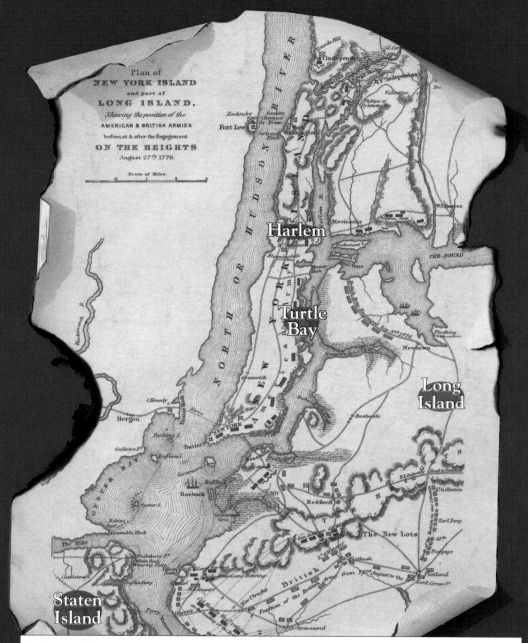

Plan of
NEW YORK ISLAND
and part of
LONG ISLAND,
Shewing the position of the
AMERICAN & BRITISH ARMIES
before, at & after the Engagement
ON THE HEIGHTS
August 27th 1776.

New York was an active battleground during the summer of 1776. In July, the British took over Staten Island. On August 27, they attacked and defeated American troops in the Battle of Long Island. Shortly after this, the Americans were forced back to Harlem Heights, and Nathan Hale sneaked behind British lines on Long Island.

A City Is Lost

N ow, as I sit in my jail cell, I think about the events of the last few days. I was captured last night. I had spent over a week on Long Island and then in New York City without being caught. My disguise as a schoolmaster was perfect. I wore plain clothes and looked nothing like a soldier.

I sneaked into the British camps on Long Island. I was able to draw maps and pictures of these camps. I took careful notes about their army that would surely help Commander Washington. I wrote the notes in Latin, a language I learned in school. I hid my notes in my shoes. For a few days, I continued to work and stayed out of sight.

It was the third night of my mission on Long Island when I heard British soldiers cheering. They shouted that the British had taken New

York City. General Howe had attacked the patriot army and won. But how could they have done it so quickly? The soldiers said that Howe was in New York City at the Beekman Mansion in Turtle Bay. The patriots had been forced north to Harlem Heights.

I was filled with sadness. I couldn't believe we had lost New York City. My mission was over. My fellow patriots were only a few miles north of me. Part of me wanted to leave Long Island and join them in Harlem Heights. But I thought of another way to continue my mission. I decided I would sneak across the East River and enter New York City. There, I would find out what the British were planning next. I carefully thought how I would get to Beekman Mansion in Turtle Bay to spy on the British.

I waited until early morning so I would not be seen. I made my way to Brooklyn and then took a ferryboat to New York City. I walked through the streets in my plain clothes. I had to be very careful. Now that the British had con-

trol of the city, their soldiers were everywhere. I found an inn and slept for a few hours. I planned to go to Turtle Bay the next morning.

I woke up to a strong smell of smoke. People were running about outside my window. They were shouting that lower New York City was burning. Could it be true? I got up to talk to other people at the inn. They said that Commander Washington had ordered the patriots to set New York City on fire. Some people in the street shouted, "Hang the patriots!" It was very unsafe for me now. I knew I had to reach my friends in Harlem Heights.

But could I get there withought being caught by the British?

During the night of September 20, 1776, a fire broke out in the lower part of New York City. Some people believe the fire was started by the order of Genereal Washington to throw off the British. The fire made the British angry.

Chapter Four

CAPTURED

*T*he fires burned on. Yet I had to get to the patriots in Harlem Heights. If Commander Washington *did* order the city set on fire, I had to find out what he planned to do next. Surely he must have a new plan to win the war. I wanted to be a part of it. I left at sunset.

After walking about a mile, I came across a field of weapons hidden behind a group of trees. It was a British campsite! I quickly took notes and started to draw a map of what I saw. I would bring them to Washington to help him plan our next move. I thought about how helpful this could be as I finished the map. Then, all of the sudden, there were footsteps behind me. I was afraid to turn around.

My hands started to shake. Sweat slid down the sides of my face. This was it—the moment I had feared since I started my mission. The British soldiers had spotted me. I felt as though my heart might burst through my chest. I quickly slipped the drawing into my pocket.

I turned around. I was face to face with a gun. The cold edge of it was an inch from my neck. Several soldiers surrounded me. The soldier holding the gun screamed, "What is your name?" I knew I had to stay calm.

"I am Nathan Hale, sir," I replied.

He looked me up and down and continued, "What are you doing here?"

"I am here looking for work as a teacher," I said. I held my breath and tried to look like I was telling the truth. Would they believe me?

A soldier was ordered to look through my pockets. As he reached toward me, I knew he would find the map. He pulled it out, laughed

at me and said, "Ah, you must be an art teacher!" He was making fun of the story I told. They knew I was not a teacher. The soldiers began searching me. I was ordered to take off my hat, shoes, and jacket. I knew it was over. The soldiers found the rest of my hidden drawings and notes.

I took a deep breath and said, "I am here to gather knowledge about your army. I am Captain Nathan Hale of the American army."

The soldiers grabbed me. I was taken to Turtle Bay to meet General Howe. My hands and feet had been put in heavy chains. I was in great pain as the soldiers led me into Howe's office. I bled as the chains cut into my skin, but I was not scared. I would be proud to tell General Howe of Commander Washington and the patriot army. He should know his fight to keep the British rule over the colonies would not be an easy one!

Captain Nathan Hale was hanged on September 22, 1776 for spying on the British. His famous last words, "I only regret that I have but one life to lose for my country," show how proud and brave a soldier he was. This hand-colored drawing shows Hale moments before the British ended his life.

Chapter Five

But One Life

When General Howe asked who I was, I explained my purpose with my head held high. "I am Nathan Hale, sir. I am a captain in the American army. I serve my Commander George Washington and my fellow patriots."

General Howe nodded. The officers handed him my papers and drawings. He looked at them closely. "These are perfect field notes," he said. He thought for a moment and looked up at me. "Might we ask you to join *our* cause? Your skills would be welcomed in the British army," he said. I could not believe my ears. How dare Howe ask me to turn against my brothers—and my promise to fight for independence!

I looked at him and repeated, "I serve my commander George Washington and my fellow

patriots." This made Howe angry. His face turned red and his brow began to sweat.

With his voice deep and dark, he screamed, "Then you will hang having done so, Captain Hale!" He turned to the other officers and continued to yell, "I have found this prisoner to be a spy for the enemy. He shall be hung tomorrow morning at eleven o'clock!"

I was taken to a jail cell near the Beekman Mansion. Guards stood around it to make sure I would not escape. It was in this cell that I spent my long night without sleep. During this night I thought about my fate. I wondered what America would be like when the war ended. I hoped that my nephews and nieces would be raised in an America free of England. I smiled when I thought about the sweet feeling of winning the war against the British. It gave me the strength to face what waited for me the next day—the day that would mark my place in history.

Now that day—September 22, 1776—is here.

William Cunningham comes into my cell. "Stand!" he demands. Officers tie my hands behind my back. They prepare me for the hanging and lead me outside. There is a large group of soldiers up ahead, next to a line of apple trees. A rope is swinging from one of the biggest trees. There is a ladder beneath it.

We march to that tree. I am forced around to face the crowd. Cunningham speaks loudly to the gathering of soldiers. "A spy among us, he was caught. A spy he will die, before our very eyes," Cunningham says as he laughs. I am angry. I will not let this monster have his fun. I will die as a proud patriot and show the British soldiers the power of the American spirit!

"Climb, fool," Cunningham shouts as he pushes me toward the ladder.

I smile at him and say as loudly as I can, "I take these next steps with great pride." The crowd is silent. They look shocked. Cunningham stops smiling. There is a wild look in his eyes. I know my pride is making

him angry. He shoves me onto the ladder and I fall hard. I feel blood drip down my face.

"Get up there before I shoot you," he warns.

I climb without the aid of my hands. A voice from the crowd shouts, "Do you not know you will soon die? How can you be so calm?"

"Of course I know that I will die," I say. "I have done as every good officer should do—I have followed my commander's orders. Whether they lead me to death or to life, I do not care. Either way, they lead me to liberty."

I reach the top of the wooden ladder. A British soldier stands next to me on another ladder. He places the rope around my neck and asks me, "So patriot, you have no regrets?"

"I have but one," I say. "I only regret that I have but one life to lose for my country."

The last words I hear are Cunningham's: "Swing him off!"

GLOSSARY

college (KOL-ij) a place where students can study after they have finished high school

colonist (KOL-uh-nist) someone who lives in a newly settled area

disguise (diss-GIZE) clothes that hide your identity

execution (EK-suh-kyoo-shun) killing someone as punishment for a crime

independence (in-di-PEN-duhnss) freedom

patriot (PAY-tree-uht) someone who loves his or her country and is prepared to fight for it

protect (pruh-TEKT) to guard or keep something safe from harm, attack, or injury

regret (ri-GRET) to be sad or sorry about something

silhouette (sil-oo-ET) a dark outline seen against a light background

spy (SPYE) someone, especially a government agent, who secretly collects information about an enemy

volunteered (vol-uhn-TEERD) to offer to do a job, usually without pay

Primary Sources

We can learn about the people, places, and events of Nathan Hale's time by looking for the right clues. These clues can be found in old documents, letters, diaries, paintings, and other items. For example, by reading the words of the patriots in the Declaration of Independence, shown on page 30, we learn why the colonists wanted to create a new nation. Studying the Declaration of Independence helps us explain the causes of the Revolutionary War.

Primary sources help us to imagine what life was like for Hale at this time. Letters, such as the one on page 29, give us details about the American army. Hale wrote this letter to his brother to tell him about the war and to ask about his family. By reading Hale's letter, we can identify the important things he was thinking about while fighting for freedom. Sources such as the Declaration of Independence and Hale's letter answer our questions about what happened in the past and why.

which compleats the Company.

We are hardly able to judge as to the number the British army for the Summer is to consist of — undoubted sufficient to cause us too much bloodshed.

Gen.l Washington is at the Congrs. being sent for thither to advice on matters of Consequence.

I had written you a compleat letter.

This is part of a letter that Hale wrote to his brother, Enoch, from New York City, on June 3, 1776. The letter describes the growing strength of the American army and Commander Washington at a meeting with the Continental Congress.

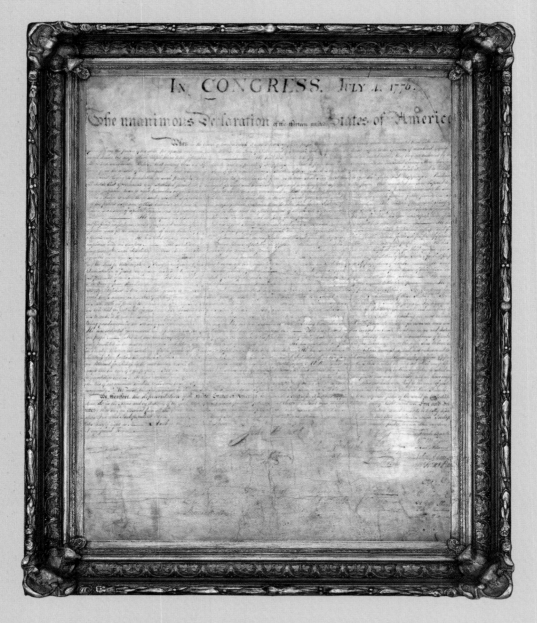

The Declaration of Independence was written in 1776. It announced the freedom of the thirteen colonies from England. It was approved by the Continental Congress on July 4, 1776, about three months before Nathan Hale's capture and execution.

Nathan Hale was promoted to the rank of captain in the American army in the spring of 1776. He was selected to be a member of a special team of soldiers, known as Knowlton's Rangers. Commander Washington asked the leader of the Rangers to find a man skilled enough for a daring spy mission. Only Hale volunteered. Shown above is Hale's signature.

Nathan Hale grew up in Coventry, Connecticut. Pictured above is a silhouette of Hale's head, which was traced on a door in his family's house. This silhouette has helped many artists create statues and portraits of Hale.